To Pavla, an author with brilliant ideas, an amazingly thorough editor, and the kindest and most caring colleague and friend. We were honored to know you.

Our Cat's Day

Albatros

Pleased to meet you

This is a young tomcat.
Neither a full-grown cat
nor an itsy-bitsy kitten.
A young cat.
Call him what you like.

That's right.
Think of a name for him.
Go on!

And what is your name?

Good morning!

Only cats and kittens can do this. And people who copy them.

Arch your back.
Push your spine up,
then pull it down.

Forget to meow,
though—it won't work.
Good morning!

Can you arch your back too?

First,
to the toilet!

Cats are
clean animals.
For them, a home toilet
is just the thing.

Not a flush toilet, of course!
A cat's toilet is a tray
with special sand in it.
We change the sand often.

Do you know how to clean a cat's toilet?

Let's wash!

Every morning
our cat and I must wash.
I wash my face, brush my teeth,
and comb my hair.

Our cat cleans his fur.
He has the right kind
of tongue for it.

And you, do you like water on your face?

Breakfast sets you up for the day

Our cat is hungry. On his plate
is meat from a pouch.
This bowl is for water,
this one for biscuits.

Yum! He's eaten it all
but wishes he hadn't.

What are you having?

Fresh air

Time to go out.
The garden is both
a meadow and a jungle.

There's so much
to see here. So much
to smell! We run around
and play.

Can you find all the cats in the garden?

First successes

What's that you've got,
little cat? A dead bird?
A mouse?

It's your first catch.
I can see you're proud of it.

At last I've learned
to tie my shoelaces.
Yuy!

What have you
achieved today?

Let's play inside

I have my toys,
our cat has his.

Cat toys are easy to make.
Sometimes all you need
is a ball of wool.

We lend each other toys.
Look, it's our cat's ball!

What are your favorite toys?

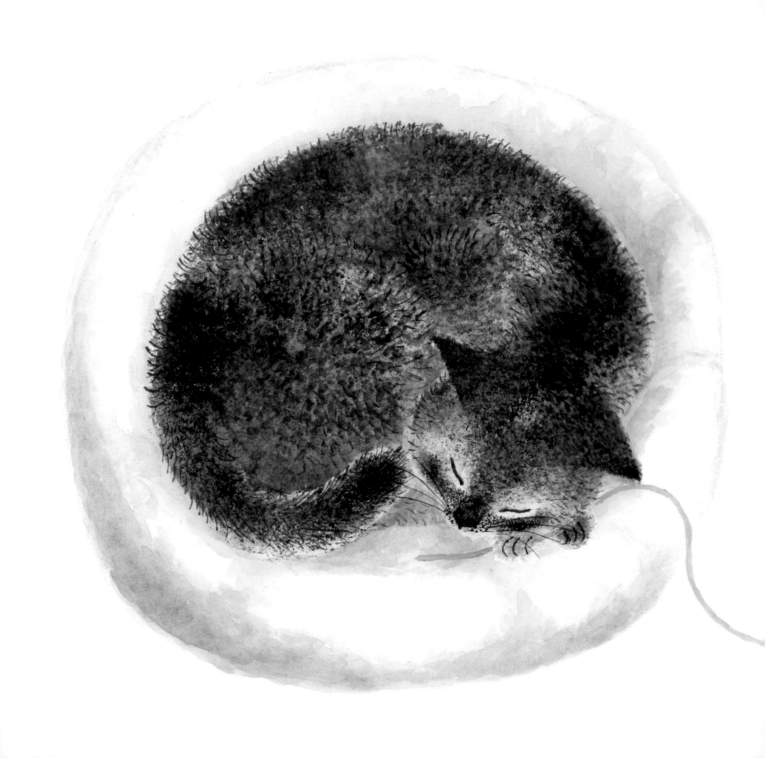

Afternoon
rest time

Rest is important too.
Our cat wiggles
in his sleep.

Maybe he's dreaming
of cat paradise, where
he's always being
fed delicious treats.

How do you take a rest?

The care of a friend

They say cats have nine lives.
Our cat has only one.

We care for him well.
No ticks or fleas on him!

And no worms
in his tummy.
His fur is lovely
and soft.

How do you take care of yourself?

Trouble

Our cat gets up to
mischief. He climbs
wherever he likes.

He knocks over
valuable things,
then pretends
it wasn't him.

What should you do when you break something?

Evening
cuddle time

It's evening. Hear that?
Our cat is purring
contentedly.

When he purrs in my arms,
it's the best thing ever.
It's cuddle time.
How happy we are together!

Who do you like to cuddle with?

Goodnight!

It's time to go to sleep. Our cat in his basket, me in my bed. He crawls in with me, and I let him stay.

He's like the softest pillow.
Cats love sleep. They sleep
when people don't.
They're little beasts.

What will you dream about tonight?

Assembly
of cats

We like to think our
cat lives alone.

But when the moon is out,
lots of other cats come around.
Every cat is different.
Every cat is beautiful.
Our cat is never alone.

Conor

Kitty

These cats are hiding on some pages in this book!

Archie

Sabine

Maya

Loki

Lady

Dora

Dopey

Lawrence

Can you find them all?

Sophie

Max

Our Cat's Day

© B4U Publishing for Albatros,
an imprint of Albatros Media Group, 2023
5. května 1746/22, Prague 4, Czech Republic
Written by Radek Malý
Illustrated by Iku Dekune
Translated by Andrew Oakland
Edited by Scott Alexander Jones
www.albatrosbooks.com